foreword

An air of mystery surrounds mushrooms. They seem to pop up overnight on lawns and forest floors, and any child can tell you that they make perfect umbrellas for elves and other woodland creatures.

But what really makes edible mushrooms magical is their adaptability. You can stuff them for appetizers, simmer them in soups, slice them into sides and toss them into entrees. And depending on how they're cooked, these fabulous fungi will even change their texture. Compare, for instance, their earthy firmness in our Brie-Filled Mushrooms with their silky succulence in our Creamy Wild Mushrooms on Pastry Points.

We're wild about mushrooms at Company's Coming, so we hunted through our cookbooks for some of our favourite recipes. Whether it's a Porcini-Rubbed Beef Roast or Mushroom Dill Muffins, you'll quickly fall under the spell of *Mushroom Magic*.

Jean Paré

creamy eggs on mushrooms

No electric grill? Broil these breakfast mushrooms on a greased broiler pan 4 inches (10 cm) from the heat for about five minutes a side until tender.

Olive (or cooking) oil	2 tbsp.	30 mL
Garlic clove, minced	1	1
Large portobello mushrooms (about 5 inch, 12.5 cm, diameter), stems removed	4	4
Olive (or cooking) oil	1 tbsp.	15 mL
Chopped onion	1/2 cup	125 mL
Diced red pepper	1/2 cup	125 mL
Garlic clove, minced	1	1
All-purpose flour	4 tsp.	20 mL
Low-sodium prepared chicken broth	2/3 cup	150 mL
Whipping cream	1/4 cup	60 mL
Large hard-cooked eggs, chopped	4	4
Seasoned salt	1/2 tsp.	2 mL
Dried dillweed	1/4 tsp.	1 mL
Pepper	1/8 tsp.	0.5 mL
Finely chopped fresh parsley	1 tbsp.	15 mL

Combine first amounts of olive oil and garlic in small cup.

Remove and discard dark gills from mushrooms with spoon. Brush olive oil mixture on both sides of mushrooms. Preheat electric grill for 5 minutes. Cook mushrooms on greased grill for about 5 minutes per side until grill marks appear and mushrooms are tender. Transfer to large plate. Cover to keep warm.

Heat second amount of olive oil in large frying pan on medium. Add onion. Cook for about 5 minutes, stirring often, until softened.

Add red pepper and second amount of garlic. Cook for 2 to 3 minutes, stirring often, until red pepper is tender-crisp.

Add flour. Heat and stir for 1 minute.

Slowly add broth and whipping cream, stirring constantly until smooth. Heat and stir for about 5 minutes until boiling and thickened.

Add next 4 ingredients. Stir until heated through. Spoon egg mixture onto mushroom caps.

Sprinkle with parsley. Makes 4 stuffed mushrooms.

1 stuffed mushroom: 279 Calories; 21.4 g Total Fat (11.1 g Mono, 2.0 g Poly, 6.3 g Sat); 234 mg Cholesterol; 13 g Carbohydrate; 3 g Fibre; 11 g Protein; 330 mg Sodium

prosciutto and mushroom omelette

*Lazy weekends beg for hearty breakfasts with a handful of ingredients
—make sure the fridge is stocked Friday night so you can have a leisurely
Saturday morning.*

Cooking oil	1 tbsp.	15 mL
Sliced fresh brown (or white) mushrooms	2 cups	500 mL
Chopped prosciutto (or deli) ham	3 oz.	85 g
Large eggs	6	6
Chopped fresh parsley (or 1 tbsp., 15 mL, flakes)	1/4 cup	60 mL
Salt	1/4 tsp.	1 mL
Pepper	1/4 tsp.	1 mL
Grated sharp white Cheddar cheese	1/2 cup	125 mL

Heat cooking oil in large frying pan on medium. Add mushrooms. Cook
for about 5 minutes, stirring occasionally, until golden.

Add prosciutto. Heat and stir for about 5 minutes until prosciutto starts
to crisp.

Whisk next 4 ingredients in small bowl until frothy. Add to mushroom
mixture. Stir. Reduce heat to medium-low. Cook for 3 to 5 minutes until
almost set.

Sprinkle with cheese. Cook, covered, for 2 to 3 minutes until cheese is
melted. Fold omelette in half. Cuts into 6 wedges.

1 wedge: 224 Calories; 17.7 g Total Fat (7.6 g Mono, 2.3 g Poly, 6.3 g Sat);
238 mg Cholesterol; 2 g Carbohydrate; trace Fibre; 14 g Protein; 452 mg Sodium

seta antojitos especial

Portobello and Madeira—a fortified wine—add richness and body to wraps that slice into decadent finger food. Madeira hails from an island of the same name and is often served as an aperitif or dessert wine. It pairs exceptionally well with cheese.

Olive oil	1 tbsp.	15 mL
Chopped fresh portobello mushrooms	4 cups	1 L
Chopped leek (white part only)	1/2 cup	125 mL
Salt	1/4 tsp.	1 mL
Pepper	1/4 tsp.	1 mL
Madeira wine	2 tbsp.	30 mL
Chopped fresh thyme	1 1/2 tsp.	7 mL
Grated havarti cheese	1 1/2 cups	375 mL
Flour tortillas (9 inch, 22 cm, diameter)	2	2

Sprigs of fresh thyme, for garnish

Heat olive oil in large frying pan on medium-high. Add next 4 ingredients. Cook for about 10 minutes, stirring occasionally, until mushrooms are browned and liquid is evaporated.

Add wine and thyme. Cook, stirring occasionally until wine is evaporated. Remove from heat.

Add cheese. Stir. Spread mushroom mixture over tortillas, leaving 1/2 inch (12 mm) border. Roll up to enclose. Arrange, seam-side down, on greased baking sheet. Bake in 400°F (205°C) oven until browned and cheese is melted. Let stand for 2 minutes. Trim ends. Cut each diagonally into 5 slices.

Garnish with thyme sprigs. Makes 10 slices.

1 slice: 199 Calories; 14.4 g Total Fat (1.0 g Mono, 0.1 g Poly, 8.9 g Sat); 30 mg Cholesterol; 7 g Carbohydrate; 1 g Fibre; 7 g Protein; 306 mg Sodium

creamy wild mushrooms on pastry points

The wild mushroom varieties give this dish an earthy flavour, but even the mild notes of white button mushrooms would stand out in this elegant but easy appetizer.

Package of puff pastry (14 oz., 397 g), thawed according to package directions	1/2	1/2
Butter	2 tbsp.	30 mL
Chopped fresh shiitake mushrooms	3 cups	750 mL
Chopped fresh oyster mushrooms	2 cups	500 mL
Finely chopped onion	1/3 cup	75 mL
Garlic clove, minced	1	1
Salt	1/4 tsp.	1 mL
Pepper	1/8 tsp.	0.5 mL
Whipping cream	2/3 cup	150 mL
Dry sherry	3 tbsp.	50 mL
Chopped fresh thyme	1/2 tsp.	2 mL

Sprigs of fresh thyme, for garnish

Roll out puff pastry on lightly floured surface to 12 x 5 inch (30 x 12.5 cm) rectangle. Cut crosswise into 6 rectangles. Cut rectangles diagonally to form triangles. Arrange on ungreased baking sheet. Bake in 400°F (205°C) oven for 15 to 20 minutes until golden. Let stand on sheet on wire rack until cool.

Melt butter in large frying pan on medium-high. Add next 6 ingredients. Cook for about 15 minutes, stirring often, until onion is softened and mushrooms are browned.

Add next 3 ingredients. Cook, stirring occasionally, until heated through. Serve over pastry.

Garnish with thyme sprigs. Serves 6.

1 serving: 288 Calories; 22.2 g Total Fat (3.7 g Mono, 0.5 g Poly, 10.6 g Sat); 44 mg Cholesterol; 17 g Carbohydrate; 2 g Fibre; 5 g Protein; 307 mg Sodium

brie-filled mushrooms

Easily doubled, this hot appetizer can be prepared earlier in the day. When you're ready for the first course, remove from the fridge and heat as directed.

Extra-large fresh whole white mushrooms (about 2 1/2 inch, 6.4 cm, diameter), stems removed	12	12
Bacon slices, cooked crisp and crumbled	4	4
Jellied cranberry sauce	1/4 cup	60 mL
Brie cheese round, cut into 12 equal pieces	4 oz.	125 g

Pepper, sprinkle

Arrange mushroom caps, stem-side up, in single layer on greased baking sheet with sides. Stuff next 3 ingredients, in order given, on mushroom caps. Bake in 400°F (205°C) oven for about 15 minutes until mushrooms are tender and cheese is melted.

Sprinkle with pepper. Makes 12 mushrooms. Serves 4.

1 serving: 196 Calories; 12.2 g Total Fat (4.0 g Mono, 0.8 g Poly, 6.6 g Sat); 37 mg Cholesterol; 12 g Carbohydrate; 2 g Fibre; 11 g Protein; 307 mg Sodium

chèvre-stuffed mushrooms

The sweet/savoury, creamy/crunchy contrasts make this an intriguing start to an intimate dinner for two. And since this recipe is happily doubled or tripled, it's also great finger food for a crowd.

Soft goat (chèvre) cheese, cut up	3 tbsp.	50 mL
Chopped dried cranberries	2 tbsp.	30 mL
Chopped pecans, toasted (see Tip, page 64)	1 tbsp.	15 mL
Pepper	1/8 tsp.	0.5 mL
Fresh whole white mushrooms (2 inch, 5 cm diameter), stems removed	6	6

Combine first 4 ingredients in small bowl.

Arrange mushroom caps in greased pie plate. Spoon cheese mixture into mushroom caps. Bake in 400°F (205°C) oven for about 15 minutes until mushrooms are tender and filling starts to brown. Let stand for 1 minute. Makes 6 stuffed mushrooms. Serves 2.

1 serving: 101 Calories; 5.8 g Total Fat (2.2 g Mono, 1.0 g Poly, 2.3 g Sat); 6 mg Cholesterol; 9 g Carbohydrate; 1 g Fibre; 5 g Protein; 55 mg Sodium

mushroom risotto balls

Follow our deep-frying tip, page 64, for lovely, crispy appetizers.

Cooking oil	1 tsp.	5 mL
Finely chopped fresh white mushrooms	1 cup	250 mL
Finely chopped onion	1/2 cup	125 mL
Arborio rice	1/2 cup	125 mL
Dry (or alcohol-free) white wine	1/4 cup	60 mL
Hot prepared vegetable broth	1 1/3 cups	325 mL
Pepper	1/4 tsp.	1 mL
Grated Parmesan cheese	1/4 cup	60 mL
Grated lemon zest	1/2 tsp.	2 mL
All-purpose flour	2 tbsp.	30 mL
Asiago cheese cubes (1/2 inch, 12 mm, each)	12	12
Cooking oil	3 cups	750 mL
Prepared rosé pasta sauce, warmed	1/2 cup	125 mL

Sprigs of fresh parsley, for garnish

Heat first amount of cooking oil in medium saucepan on medium. Add mushrooms and onion. Cook for about 10 minutes, stirring often, until softened. Add rice. Heat and stir for 30 seconds.

Add wine. Cook, stirring occasionally, until wine is almost evaporated. Add broth and pepper. Bring to a boil. Reduce heat to medium-low. Simmer, covered, for about 15 minutes, without stirring, until rice is tender and liquid is absorbed.

Add Parmesan cheese and lemon zest. Stir. Spoon 12 portions of risotto mixture onto waxed paper-lined baking sheet. Let stand for about 5 minutes until cool.

Put flour into small bowl. Place 1 Asiago cheese cube on risotto portion. With wet hands, roll into ball, enclosing cheese. Toss ball in flour until lightly coated. Repeat with remaining risotto portions, cheese cubes and flour.

Heat second amount of cooking oil in a large frying pan on medium-high. Shallow-fry risotto balls in 375°F (190°C) oil for 2 to 3 minutes, turning occasionally, until golden and heated through. Transfer to paper towel-lined plate. Let stand for 2 minutes.

Drizzle pasta sauce on serving plate. Arrange risotto balls over sauce.

Garnish with parsley. Makes 12 risotto balls.

1 risotto ball: 105 Calories; 6.9 g Total Fat (1.1 g Mono, 0.5 g Poly, 3.4 g Sat); 16 mg Cholesterol; 5 g Carbohydrate; trace Fibre; 5 g Protein; 300 mg Sodium

hot mushroom dip

If your schedule is full on the day of the party, stir everything together and spread into a heatproof dish up to two days before. Cover and refrigerate until you pop it into the oven. Fresh vegetables, crackers and pita wedges make great dippers.

Hard margarine (or butter)	2 tbsp.	30 mL
Chopped fresh white mushrooms	3 cups	750 mL
Finely chopped onion	1 cup	250 mL
Garlic clove, minced (or 1/4 tsp., 1 mL, powder), optional	1	1
Cream cheese, softened and cut up	8 oz.	250 g
Dried dillweed	1/2 tsp.	2 mL
Seasoned salt	1/2 tsp.	2 mL
Pepper, sprinkle		
Grated jalapeño Monterey Jack cheese	1 1/2 cups	375 mL
Mayonnaise	1/2 cup	125 mL
Sliced fresh white mushrooms, for garnish		

Chopped fresh chives, for garnish

Melt margarine in large frying pan on medium. Add next 3 ingredients. Cook for about 10 minutes, stirring occasionally, until mushrooms are golden and liquid is evaporated. Remove from heat.

Add next 4 ingredients. Stir until cream cheese is melted.

Add Monterey Jack cheese and mayonnaise. Mix well. Spread into ungreased 9 inch (22 cm) pie plate or shallow casserole. Sprinkle with sliced mushrooms. Bake in 350°F (175°C) oven for about 30 minutes until heated through.

Garnish with chives. Makes about 2 1/2 cups (625 mL).

2 tbsp. (30 mL): 131 Calories; 12.5 g Total Fat (5.2 g Mono, 1.9 g Poly, 4.9 g Sat); 24 mg Cholesterol; 2 g Carbohydrate; trace Fibre; 3 g Protein; 153 mg Sodium

mushroom tarts

Make these up to three months ahead of time. Just add the cooled filling to the baked, cooled shells and freeze. Reheat thawed tarts at 325°F (160°C) for 15 to 20 minutes (or 30 to 40 minutes if frozen) until heated.

Hard margarine (or butter)	1 tbsp.	15 mL
Chopped fresh white mushrooms	1 cup	250 mL
Chopped green onion	1 tbsp.	15 mL
All-purpose flour	2 tbsp.	30 mL
Salt	1/4 tsp.	1 mL
Skim evaporated milk (or half-and-half cream)	2/3 cup	150 mL
Frozen mini tart shells, thawed	18	18

Melt margarine in medium saucepan on medium. Add mushrooms and green onion. Cook for 5 to 10 minutes, stirring often, until mushrooms are golden.

Add flour and salt. Heat and stir for 1 minute.

Slowly add evaporated milk, stirring constantly. Heat and stir until boiling and thickened. Let stand until cool.

Arrange mini tart shells on ungreased baking sheet. Bake in 400°F (205°C) oven for 10 to 13 minutes until lightly browned. Let stand until cool. Spoon mushroom mixture into tart shells. Bake for about 5 minutes until hot. Makes 18 tarts.

1 tart: 53 Calories; 3.0 g Total Fat (1.6 g Mono, 0.6 g Poly, 0.7 g Sat); trace Cholesterol; 5 g Carbohydrate; trace Fibre; 1 g Protein; 100 mg Sodium

miso soup

Fungus fans can appreciate their favourite food year round when the mushrooms are dried. Rinse them well in a strainer under cold water to remove any grit before plumping them up, and be sure to save the hot water—it's full of flavour.

Dried shiitake mushrooms	3	3
Boiling water	1 cup	250 mL
Miso (fermented soybean paste)	1/4 cup	60 mL
Sesame (or cooking) oil	2 tsp.	10 mL
Green onions, sliced	3	3
Coarsely shredded carrot	1/4 cup	60 mL
Water	3 cups	750 mL
Firm tofu, cut into 1/2 inch (12 mm) pieces	5 oz.	140 g
Fresh bean sprouts	1 cup	250 mL
Green onion, sliced	1	1
Sesame seeds, toasted (see Tip, page 64)	1 1/2 tsp.	7 mL

Put mushrooms into small heatproof bowl. Add boiling water. Stir. Let stand for 20 minutes until softened. Strain through sieve lined with paper towel or several layers of cheesecloth, reserving liquid. Remove and discard stems. Slice mushrooms very thinly. Set aside.

Combine reserved liquid and miso in separate small bowl. Set aside.

Heat sesame oil in medium saucepan on medium. Add first amount of green onion and carrot. Cook for about 2 minutes until softened.

Add water, mushrooms and miso mixture. Bring to a boil. Add tofu. Reduce heat to medium-low. Simmer, covered, for 3 minutes.

Just before serving, sprinkle with remaining 3 ingredients. Serves 6.

1 serving: 90 Calories; 4.8 g Total Fat (1.4 g Mono, 2.4 g Poly, 0.7 g Sat); 0 mg Cholesterol; 8 g Carbohydrate; 2 g Fibre; 6 g Protein; 452 mg Sodium

cream of mushroom soup

If you're disheartened by the mush in canned mushroom soup, here's an antidote: mushroom slices, a medley of seasonings and the tang of wine and sour cream make this an event.

Butter (or hard margarine)	2 tbsp.	30 mL
Thinly sliced fresh brown (or white) mushrooms	10 cups	2.5 L
Finely chopped onion	2 1/2 cups	625 mL
Chopped fresh dill (or 1 tbsp., 15 mL, dried)	1/4 cup	60 mL
Butter (or hard margarine)	1 tbsp.	15 mL
Paprika	2 tsp.	10 mL
Salt	1/2 tsp.	2 mL
Pepper	1/4 tsp.	1 mL
All-purpose flour	1/4 cup	60 mL
Prepared chicken (or vegetable) broth	3 cups	750 mL
Dry (or alcohol-free) white wine	1/2 cup	125 mL
Half-and-half cream	1 cup	250 mL
Chopped fresh parsley	3 tbsp.	50 mL
Sour cream	1/4 cup	60 mL
Lemon juice	1 1/2 tbsp.	25 mL

Melt first amount of butter in large saucepan on medium-high. Add mushrooms. Cook for about 10 minutes, stirring often, until mushrooms are browned and liquid is evaporated.

Add next 6 ingredients. Heat and stir on medium until second amount of butter is melted. Cook, covered, for 5 to 10 minutes, stirring occasionally, until onion is softened.

Sprinkle with flour. Heat and stir for 1 minute. Slowly add 2 cups (500 mL) broth. Heat and stir until boiling and thickened. Add remaining broth and wine. Stir. Bring to a boil. Reduce heat to medium-low. Simmer, covered, for 15 minutes, stirring occasionally, to blend flavours.

Add half-and-half cream and parsley. Stir.

Combine sour cream and lemon juice in small cup. Drizzle over individual servings. Makes about 7 cups (1.75 L).

1 cup (250 mL): 188 Calories; 10.7 g Total Fat (2.9 g Mono, 0.6 g Poly, 6.5 g Sat); 28 mg Cholesterol; 17 g Carbohydrate; 3 g Fibre; 6 g Protein; 615 mg Sodium

chinese mushroom soup

Chinese dried mushrooms are also sold as dried Chinese black mushrooms or dried shiitake mushrooms. Look for them at larger grocery stores or plan a visit to an Asian market for this filling slow-cooker meal in a bowl.

Chinese dried mushrooms	15	15
Boiling water	2 cup	500 mL
Prepared chicken broth	6 cups	1.5 L
Can of shoestring-style bamboo shoots, drained	8 oz.	227 mL
Can of sliced water chestnuts, drained	8 oz.	227 mL
Rice vinegar	1/3 cup	75 mL
Soy sauce	1/4 cup	60 mL
Dried crushed chilies	1 tsp.	5 mL
Diced cooked pork	1 cup	250 mL
Sliced green onion	2 tbsp.	30 mL

Put mushrooms into small heatproof bowl. Add boiling water. Stir. Let stand for about 20 minutes until softened. Drain. Remove and discard stems. Slice thinly. Transfer to 3 1/2 to 4 quart (3.5 to 4 L) slow cooker.

Add next 6 ingredients. Stir. Cook, covered, on Low for 8 to 10 hours or on High for 4 to 5 hours.

Add pork and green onion. Stir. Cook, covered, on High for 10 to 15 minutes until heated through. Makes about 8 1/2 cups (2.1 L).

1 cup (250 mL): 117 Calories; 4.7 g Total Fat (2.0 g Mono, 0.6 g Poly, 1.6 g Sat); 14 mg Cholesterol; 10 g Carbohydrate; 3 g Fibre; 9 g Protein; 936 mg Sodium

mushroom dill muffins

Pack these dilly delights next to a container of soup or salad for a filling lunch. These muffins will freeze easily; store them in an airtight container for grab-and-go emergencies.

Butter (or hard margarine)	2 tsp.	10 mL
Chopped fresh white mushrooms	2 cups	500 mL
All-purpose flour	2 1/4 cups	550 mL
Baking powder	1 1/2 tsp.	7 mL
Dried dillweed	1 tsp.	5 mL
Baking soda	1/2 tsp.	2 mL
Pepper	1/4 tsp.	1 mL
Large eggs	2	2
Can of condensed cream of mushroom soup	10 oz.	284 mL
Butter (or hard margarine), melted	1/4 cup	60 mL
Milk	1/4 cup	60 mL
Lemon juice	2 tsp.	10 mL

Melt first amount of butter in large frying pan on medium-high. Add mushrooms. Cook for 5 to 10 minutes, stirring occasionally, until mushrooms are browned and liquid is evaporated. Let stand until cool.

Combine next 5 ingredients in large bowl. Make a well in centre.

Whisk remaining 5 ingredients in medium bowl. Add to well. Add mushrooms. Stir until just moistened. Fill 12 greased muffin cups 3/4 full. Bake in 375°F (190°C) oven for 20 to 22 minutes until wooden pick inserted in centre of muffin comes out clean. Let stand in pan for 5 minutes before removing to wire rack to cool. Makes 12 muffins.

1 muffin: 177 Calories; 7.8 g Total Fat (2.1 g Mono, 1.3 g Poly, 3.8 g Sat); 49 mg Cholesterol; 22 g Carbohydrate; 1 g Fibre; 5 g Protein; 366 mg Sodium

warm mushroom salad

It's worth having your guests seated and ready to appreciate the contrast of cool, crisp lettuce with warm, softened mushrooms sweetened with honey and spiced with garlic. Demand for this recipe will mushroom!

Liquid honey, warmed	1 tbsp.	15 mL
Red wine vinegar	1 tbsp.	15 mL
Garlic cloves, minced (or 1/2 tsp., 2 mL, powder)	2	2
Small fresh whole brown mushrooms	2 cups	500 mL
Small fresh whole white mushrooms	2 cups	500 mL
Mixed salad greens, lightly packed	4 cups	1 L
Jar of roasted red peppers, drained, blotted dry, cut into thin strips	12 oz.	340 mL
Fresh bean sprouts	1 cup	250 mL
Basil pesto	1 tbsp.	15 mL
Red wine vinegar	1 tbsp.	15 mL

Combine first 3 ingredients in large bowl. Add brown and white mushrooms. Toss until coated. Spread in single layer in greased baking sheet with sides. Bake in 450°F (230°C) oven for about 10 minutes, stirring once, until mushrooms start to soften. Return to same large bowl.

Add next 3 ingredients. Toss.

Combine pesto and second amount of vinegar in small bowl. Drizzle over mushroom mixture. Toss until coated. Serves 8.

1 serving: 48 Calories; 1.0 g Total Fat (0.4 g Mono, 0.2 g Poly, 0.1 g Sat); 0 mg Cholesterol; 9 g Carbohydrate; 2 g Fibre; 3 g Protein; 66 mg Sodium

mushroom barsotto

The earthiness of the portobellos is complemented by the heartiness of the barley in this risotto-like side or vegetarian main course. Since most soup ladles hold 4 to 6 oz. (114 to 170 mL), use one to add the broth to the barley during cooking.

Olive oil	1 tbsp.	15 mL
Chopped portobello mushrooms	5 cups	1.25 L
Prepared vegetable broth	4 cups	1 L
Water	2 cups	500 mL
Olive oil	1 tbsp.	15 mL
Chopped onion	1 cup	250 mL
Pearl barley	1 cup	250 mL
Dark (or alcohol-free) beer	3/4 cup	175 mL
Grated Asiago cheese	1/3 cup	75 mL
Pepper	1/2 tsp.	2 mL

Heat first amount of olive oil in large frying pan on medium-high. Add mushrooms. Cook for 5 to 10 minutes, stirring occasionally, until mushrooms are starting to brown and liquid is evaporated. Cover to keep warm.

Combine broth and water in medium saucepan. Bring to a boil. Reduce heat to low. Cover to keep hot.

Heat second amount of olive oil in large saucepan on medium. Add onion. Cook for about 10 minutes, stirring occasionally, until starting to soften.

Add barley. Heat and stir until coated. Add beer. Heat and stir until liquid is absorbed. Add 1/2 cup (125 mL) broth mixture. Heat and stir until liquid is almost absorbed. Repeat with remaining broth mixture, adding 1/2 cup (125 mL) at a time, until liquid is absorbed and barley is tender. Add mushrooms. Cook and stir until heated through.

Add cheese and pepper. Stir. Makes about 5 cups (1.25 L).

1 cup (250 mL): 276 Calories; 8.3 g Total Fat (4.0 g Mono, 0.7 g Poly, 2.1 g Sat); 6 mg Cholesterol; 42 g Carbohydrate; 8 g Fibre; 8 g Protein; 830 mg Sodium

mushroom spinach couscous

Here's a fast side for salmon or pork tenderloin. When choosing mushrooms, look for firm specimens that are uniformly pale in colour, and store them in your crisper in a paper bag—never in plastic.

Prepared chicken broth	3 cups	750 mL
Box of plain couscous	12 oz.	340 g
Salt	1/2 tsp.	2 mL
Butter (or hard margarine)	2 tbsp.	30 mL
Chopped onion	1/2 cup	125 mL
Garlic clove, minced	1	1
(or 1/4 tsp., 1 mL, powder)		
Sliced fresh white mushrooms	2 cups	500 mL
Boxes of frozen chopped	2	2
spinach (10 oz., 300 g, each),		
thawed and squeezed dry		
Prepared chicken broth	1/4 cup	60 mL
Dried tarragon	1 tsp.	5 mL

Pour first amount of broth into medium saucepan. Bring to a boil. Add couscous and salt. Stir. Cover. Remove from heat. Let stand for about 5 minutes, without stirring, until broth is absorbed. Fluff with fork. Set aside.

Melt butter in large frying pan on medium. Add onion and garlic. Cook for 2 to 3 minutes, stirring often, until onion starts to soften.

Add mushrooms. Cook for 5 to 10 minutes, stirring occasionally, until mushrooms are softened.

Add couscous and remaining 3 ingredients. Heat and stir for 2 to 3 minutes until heated through. Serves 8.

1 serving: 227 Calories; 4.1 g Total Fat (1.1 g Mono, 0.5 g Poly, 2.1 g Sat); 8 mg Cholesterol; 38 g Carbohydrate; 4 g Fibre; 10 g Protein; 563 mg Sodium

fried rice

Chinese dried mushrooms, available at large grocery stores or Asian markets, add a meaty taste and texture to this colourful, low-fat dish.

Chinese dried mushrooms	6	6
Boiling water	2 cups	500 mL
Cooking oil	2 tsp.	10 mL
Finely chopped red pepper	1/2 cup	125 mL
Chopped green onion	1/3 cup	75 mL
Cooked long-grain white rice (1 cup, 250 mL, uncooked)	3 cups	750 mL
Frozen peas	1/2 cup	125 mL
Low-sodium soy sauce	2 tbsp.	30 mL
Chili powder	1/2 tsp.	2 mL
Finely chopped fat-free cooked ham (optional)	1/3 cup	75 mL
Fresh bean sprouts	1 1/2 cups	375 mL

Put mushrooms into small heatproof bowl. Add boiling water. Stir. Let stand for about 20 minutes until softened. Drain. Remove and discard stems. Finely chop caps. Set aside.

Heat wok or large frying pan on medium. Add cooking oil. Add red pepper and green onion. Stir-fry for about 1 minute until green onion is softened.

Add mushrooms and next 5 ingredients. Stir-fry for about 5 minutes until hot.

Add bean sprouts. Stir-fry for about 1 minute until heated through. Makes about 6 cups (1.5 L).

1 cup (250 mL): 192 Calories; 2.1 g Total Fat (1.0 g Mono, 0.6 g Poly, 0.2 g Sat); 0 mg Cholesterol; 38 g Carbohydrate; 2 g Fibre; 5 g Protein; 184 mg Sodium

mushroomed potatoes

Brown mushrooms, often called cremini or baby portobellos, are closely related to the common white mushroom, but have a bit more flavour. They'll make these mashed potatoes a main focus of any meal.

Peeled potatoes, cut up	2 lbs.	900 g
Salt	1 tsp.	5 mL
Milk	1/4 cup	60 mL
Hard margarine (or butter)	2 tbsp.	30 mL
Minced onion flakes	1 tbsp.	15 mL
Garlic cloves, minced (or 1/2 tsp., 2 mL, powder)	2	2
Chopped fresh brown (or white) mushrooms	2 cups	500 mL
Pepper, sprinkle		
Grated Swiss cheese	3/4 cup	175 mL

Pour water into large saucepan until about 1 inch (2.5 cm) deep. Add potato and salt. Cover. Bring to a boil. Reduce heat to medium. Boil gently for 12 to 15 minutes until tender. Drain. Mash.

Add milk. Beat until smooth and fluffy. Cover to keep warm.

Melt margarine in medium frying pan on medium. Add onion flakes and garlic. Heat and stir for 1 minute. Add mushrooms. Cook for about 10 minutes, stirring occasionally, until liquid is evaporated and mushrooms are golden.

Sprinkle with pepper. Add to potato. Add cheese. Mix well. Makes about 5 cups (1.25 L).

1/2 cup (125 mL): 139 Calories; 4.9 g Total Fat (2.2 g Mono, 0.4 g Poly, 2.1 g Sat); 8 mg Cholesterol; 20 g Carbohydrate; 2 g Fibre; 5 g Protein; 58 mg Sodium

nutty mushroom wild rice

White mushrooms—sometimes called supermarket mushrooms—come in three sizes: small and medium buttons, and large stuffers. Whichever you choose, their fleshy texture makes a lovely contrast to the chewy wild rice and crunchy nuts of this savoury side.

Prepared chicken broth	2 1/4 cups	550 mL
Wild rice	3/4 cup	175 mL
Butter (or hard margarine)	1 tbsp.	15 mL
Sliced fresh white mushrooms	2 cups	500 mL
Finely chopped onion	1/3 cup	75 mL
Pine nuts, toasted (see Tip, page 64)	2 tbsp.	30 mL
Slivered almonds, toasted (see Tip, page 64)	2 tbsp.	30 mL
Pepper	1/4 tsp.	1 mL

Measure broth into medium saucepan. Bring to a boil. Add rice. Stir. Reduce heat to medium-low. Cover. Simmer for about 60 minutes, without stirring, until rice is tender. Drain any remaining liquid. Transfer rice to medium bowl. Cover to keep warm.

Melt butter in medium frying pan on medium. Add mushrooms and onion. Cook for 10 to 15 minutes, stirring often, until mushrooms are browned. Add to rice.

Add remaining 3 ingredients. Toss. Makes about 3 cups (750 mL). Serves 4.

1 serving: 225 Calories; 8.7 g Total Fat (3.4 g Mono, 2.2 g Poly, 2.6 g Sat); 8 mg Cholesterol; 30 g Carbohydrate; 4 g Fibre; 8 g Protein; 862 mg Sodium

marinated mushrooms

Welcome at a picnic, on a buffet table, or in a bowl at the elbow of anyone who's mad about mushrooms, these flavourful little bites make an addictive side dish.

Water	2 cups	500 mL
Chopped onion	1/2 cup	125 mL
Lemon juice	1/3 cup	75 mL
Olive (or cooking) oil	1/4 cup	60 mL
Whole black peppercorns	1 tbsp.	15 mL
Dried oregano	2 tsp.	10 mL
Garlic cloves, minced (or 1/2 tsp., 2 mL, powder)	2	2
Bay leaves	2	2
Salt, just a pinch		
Small fresh whole white mushrooms	2 lbs.	900 g
Chopped fresh parsley	1 tbsp.	15 mL

Combine first 9 ingredients in Dutch oven or large pot. Bring to a boil on medium-high.

Add mushrooms. Cook for 5 minutes, stirring occasionally, to blend flavours. Transfer to large bowl. Let stand until cool. Let stand, covered, in refrigerator for at least 6 hours or overnight, stirring occasionally.

Transfer mushrooms with slotted spoon to medium bowl. Sprinkle with parsley. May be stored, covered, in refrigerator for up to 5 days. Serves 8.

1 serving: 64 Calories; 3.9 g Total Fat (2.5 g Mono, 0.5 g Poly, 0.5 g Sat); 0 mg Cholesterol; 7 g Carbohydrate; 2 g Fibre; 3 g Protein; 5 mg Sodium

mushroom polenta

These cornmeal-based wedges are great as a side for barbecued meats, or as a vegetarian main course—just replace the chicken broth with a vegetable one. Add a salad and some steamed green beans to complete the meal.

Cooking oil	2 tsp.	10 mL
Sliced fresh white mushrooms	2 cups	500 mL
Salt, sprinkle		
Low-sodium prepared chicken (or vegetable) broth	4 cups	1 L
Yellow cornmeal	1 1/2 cups	375 mL
Grated low-fat medium Cheddar cheese	1/2 cup	125 mL
Chopped fresh chives (or 2 1/4 tsp., 11 mL, dried)	3 tbsp.	50 mL
Pepper	1/4 tsp.	1 mL
Cooking spray		

Heat cooking oil in large saucepan on medium-high. Add mushrooms and salt. Heat and stir for about 5 minutes until mushrooms are softened and beginning to brown. Transfer to small bowl.

Pour broth into same saucepan. Bring to a boil. Reduce heat to medium-low. Slowly add cornmeal, stirring constantly. Heat and stir for about 10 minutes until mixture is thick and pulls away from side of pan.

Add mushrooms and next 3 ingredients. Stir. Spread evenly into greased 9 x 13 inch (22 x 33 cm) pan. Let stand for about 30 minutes until cool. Chill, covered, for about 1 hour until set. Cut into 12 equal wedges.

Spray both sides of polenta pieces with cooking spray. Cook in large greased frying pan, greased electric grill or gas barbecue on medium for about 3 minutes per side until lightly golden. Makes 12 wedges.

1 wedge: 100 Calories; 2.3 g Total Fat (0.9 g Mono, 0.4 g Poly, 0.8 g Sat); 4 mg Cholesterol; 15 g Carbohydrate; 1 g Fibre; 4 g Protein; 251 mg Sodium

spinach and mushroom pizza

*Gourmet pizza doesn't get any faster—just five toppings on your favourite
brand of pizza crust and 15 minutes in the oven.*

Pre-baked pizza crust (12 inch, 30 cm, diameter)	1	1
Pizza sauce	2/3 cup	150 mL
Sliced fresh white mushrooms	2 cups	500 mL
Fresh spinach leaves, lightly packed	2 cups	500 mL
Soft goat (chèvre) cheese, broken up	5 oz.	140 g
Grated Parmesan cheese	2/3 cup	150 mL

Place crust on greased pizza pan. Spread pizza sauce over crust leaving
1/2 inch (12 mm) border.

Layer remaining 4 ingredients, in order given, over pizza sauce. Bake in
500°F (260°C) oven for 12 to 15 minutes until cheese is melted and crust
is browned. Cuts into 6 wedges.

*1 wedge: 310 Calories; 14.5 g Total Fat (3.5 g Mono, 0.7 g Poly, 7.9 g Sat); 30 mg Cholesterol;
29 g Carbohydrate; 1 g Fibre; 16 g Protein; 746 mg Sodium*

seared beef with peppercorn mushrooms

This peppery, tapas-style strip loin is grilled, though you can also sear it for a minute per side in olive oil in a hot stainless steel or cast iron frying pan (non-stick coatings may be ruined with the high heat).

Chopped fresh thyme	1 tbsp.	15 mL
Montreal steak spice	1 tbsp.	15 mL
Beef strip loin steak	1 lb.	454 g
Cooking oil	1 tbsp.	15 mL
Sliced fresh brown (or white) mushrooms	5 cups	1.25 L
Brandy	1/3 cup	75 mL
Canned green peppercorns, drained	1 tbsp.	15 mL
Butter	1 tbsp.	15 ml
Arugula, lightly packed	1/2 cup	125 mL

Combine thyme and steak spice in shallow dish. Press both sides of steak into spice mixture until coated. Preheat gas barbecue to high. Cook steak on greased grill for about 2 minutes per side until browned and slightly crisp. Transfer to cutting board. Cover with foil. Let stand for 10 minutes.

Heat cooking oil in large frying pan on medium-high. Add mushrooms. Cook, stirring often, until mushrooms are browned and liquid is evaporated.

Add brandy and peppercorns. Stir. Add butter. Heat and stir until butter is melted.

Cut steak across the grain into very thin slices. Serve with mushrooms and arugula. Serves 6.

1 serving: 250 Calories; 15.7 g Total Fat (6.7 g Mono, 1.2 g Poly, 6.0 g Sat); 47 mg Cholesterol; 3 g Carbohydrate; 1 g Fibre; 17 g Protein; 391 mg Sodium

steak with mushrooms and onions

An easy marinade makes this meal a snap to prepare. You can add the flavourful stems of the portobello mushrooms to soup.

Italian dressing	1/2 cup	125 mL
Red wine vinegar	2 tbsp.	30 mL
Garlic clove, minced (or 1/4 tsp., 1 mL, powder)	1	1
Pepper, sprinkle		
Portobello mushrooms (about 4 inches, 10 cm, diameter), stems removed	2	2
Large red onion, cut into thick slices	1	1
Beef top sirloin steak	1 lb.	454 g
Seasoned salt	1/2 tsp.	2 mL
Pepper, sprinkle		

Combine first 4 ingredients in shallow dish. Set aside.

Remove and discard dark gills from mushrooms with spoon. Add mushrooms to dressing mixture. Turn until coated. Let stand in refrigerator for 30 minutes. Drain, reserving dressing mixture in small saucepan. Bring to a boil. Reduce heat to medium-low. Simmer, uncovered, for 5 minutes.

Preheat electric grill for 5 minutes or gas barbecue to medium. Arrange mushrooms and onion on greased grill. Close lid. Cook for 7 to 8 minutes, turning and basting with dressing mixture several times, until onion is tender-crisp. Transfer to medium bowl.

Arrange steak on greased grill. Cook for 1 minute per side. Sprinkle both sides with seasoned salt and pepper. Brush with dressing mixture. Close lid. Cook for 3 to 4 minutes per side until meat reaches desired doneness. Transfer to cutting board. Cover with foil. Let stand for 10 minutes. Cut across the grain into thin slices. Cut mushrooms into thin slices. Cut onion slices into quarters. Arrange mushrooms and onion over steak. Serves 4.

1 serving: 325 Calories; 23.9 g Total Fat (12.5 g Mono, 6.8 g Poly, 3.0 g Sat); 64 mg Cholesterol; 9 g Carbohydrate; 2 g Fibre; 20 g Protein; 651 mg Sodium

porcini-rubbed beef roast

Roast beef seasoned with a rub of dried porcini mushrooms, herbs and sea salt turns any meal into a celebration, especially if paired with a horseradish and roasted garlic sauce. Astoundingly good!

Package of dried porcini mushrooms	3/4 oz.	22 g
Dried thyme	2 tsp.	10 mL
Dried rosemary, crushed	1 tsp.	5 mL
Coarse sea salt	1/2 tsp.	2 mL
Beef sirloin tip roast	4 1/2 lbs.	2 kg
Fresh whole white mushrooms, stems removed	12	12
Olive oil	2 tsp.	10 mL
Sour cream	1 cup	250 mL
Roasted garlic bulb (see Tip, page 64), mashed	1	1
Prepared horseradish	1 tbsp.	15 mL
Lemon juice	2 tsp.	10 mL
Salt	1/2 tsp.	2 mL
Pepper	1/4 tsp.	1 mL

Process first 4 ingredients in blender or food processor until fine powder. Rub over roast. Let stand, covered, in refrigerator for at least 6 hours or overnight. Preheat gas barbecue to medium. Put roast on rotisserie (inset photo). Close lid. Cook for about 30 minutes until starting to brown. Reduce heat to medium-low. Cook for about 1 hour until meat thermometer inserted into thickest part of roast reads 160°F (71°C) for medium or until roast reaches desired doneness. Transfer to cutting board. Cover with foil. Let stand for 15 minutes before carving. Increase heat to medium.

Brush mushroom caps with olive oil. Arrange on greased grill. Close lid. Cook until golden.

Combine remaining 6 ingredients in small bowl. Serve with roast and mushrooms. Serves 12.

1 serving: 260 Calories; 12.8 g Total Fat (4.9 g Mono, 0.6 g Poly, 5.2 g Sat); 72 mg Cholesterol; 3 g Carbohydrate; 1 g Fibre; 31 g Protein; 269 mg Sodium

mushroom-stuffed meatloaf

Inject a little creamy mushroom magic into everyday meatloaf. Cook up a double batch; you can freeze it for up to a month.

FILLING

Hard margarine (or butter)	1 tbsp.	15 mL
Chopped fresh white mushrooms	3 cups	750 mL
Chopped onion	1 cup	250 mL
All-purpose flour	3 tbsp.	50 mL
Dried thyme	1/2 tsp.	2 mL
Salt	1/2 tsp.	2 mL
Pepper	1/4 tsp.	1 mL
Light cream cheese, cut up	4 oz.	125 g

MEAT LAYER

Large egg, fork-beaten	1	1
Fine dry bread crumbs	2/3 cup	150 mL
Milk	1/4 cup	60 mL
Low-sodium soy sauce	3 tbsp.	50 mL
Ground ginger	1/2 tsp.	2 mL
Worcestershire sauce	1/2 tsp.	2 mL
Garlic powder	1/4 tsp.	1 mL
Lean ground beef	1 1/2 lbs.	680 g

Filling: Melt margarine in large frying pan on medium-high. Add mushrooms and onion. Cook for about 10 minutes, stirring often, until onion is soft and liquid from mushrooms is evaporated. Reduce heat to medium.

Sprinkle with next 4 ingredients. Stir until combined. Add cream cheese. Heat and stir until melted. Let stand until cool.

Meat Layer: Combine first 7 ingredients in large bowl.

Add beef. Mix well. Press about 2/3 of beef mixture into bottom and 2 inches (5 cm) up sides of greased 9 x 5 x 3 inch (22 x 12.5 x 7.5 cm) loaf pan. Spoon mushroom mixture into cavity. Spread evenly. Shape remaining beef mixture to fit in pan. Place on top, smoothing and sealing sides. Bake, uncovered, in 325°F (160°C) oven for about 1 hour until fully cooked and internal temperature reaches 160°F (71°C). Serves 6.

1 serving: 416 Calories; 24.9 g Total Fat (10.6 g Mono, 1.5 g Poly, 10.1 g Sat); 113 mg Cholesterol; 19 g Carbohydrate; 2 g Fibre; 28 g Protein; 819 mg Sodium

chicken tetrazzini

Named after opera singer Luisa Tetrazzini, this casserole hits all the high notes.

Chopped cooked chicken	3 cups	750 mL
Cooked spaghetti, cut up (about 1/2 lb, 225 g, dry)	3 cups	750 mL
Cooking oil	2 tsp.	10 mL
Sliced fresh white mushrooms	2 cups	500 mL
Sliced red pepper	1/2 cup	125 mL
Sliced green onion	1/3 cup	75 mL
All-purpose flour	2 tbsp.	30 mL
Low-sodium chicken bouillon powder	2 tsp.	10 mL
Water	1 cup	250 mL
Skim evaporated milk	1/2 cup	125 mL
Grated Parmesan cheese	1/3 cup	75 mL
Medium sherry	2 tbsp.	30 mL
Salt	1/4 tsp.	1 mL
Pepper	1/8 tsp.	0.5 mL
Grated light sharp Cheddar cheese	1 cup	250 mL

Combine chicken and pasta in large bowl. Set aside.

Heat cooking oil in large frying pan on medium. Add next 3 ingredients. Cook for about 10 minutes, stirring occasionally, until red pepper is softened.

Combine flour and bouillon powder in small bowl. Slowly add water stirring constantly until smooth. Slowly add to red pepper mixture, stirring constantly. Heat and stir for about 1 minute until boiling and thickened.

Add next 5 ingredients. Stir. Add to pasta mixture. Toss. Transfer to greased 3 quart (3 L) casserole. Bake, covered, in 350°F (175°C) oven for about 30 minutes until heated through.

Sprinkle with Cheddar cheese. Bake, uncovered, for another 4 to 5 minutes until Cheddar cheese is melted. Serves 4.

1 serving: 561 Calories; 14.4 g Total Fat (4.6 g Mono, 1.9 g Poly, 6.4 g Sat); 96 mg Cholesterol; 54 g Carbohydrate; 2 g Fibre; 49 g Protein; 761 mg Sodium

scallop mushroom fettuccine

White wine, Parmesan and scallops add panache to this simple, satisfying dish. A salad or some roasted vegetables and a bottle of white wine would round out an easy, weekend dinner on the deck.

Water	12 cups	3 L
Salt	1 1/2 tsp.	7 mL
Fettuccine	8 oz.	225 g
Olive (or cooking) oil	1 tbsp.	15 mL
Sliced fresh white mushrooms	4 cups	1 L
Garlic clove, minced (or 1/4 tsp., 1 mL, powder)	1	1
Dry (or alcohol-free) white wine	1/4 cup	60 mL
Butter (or hard margarine)	2 tbsp.	30 mL
Lemon juice	1 tbsp.	15 mL
Small bay scallops	1 lb.	454 g
Grated Parmesan cheese	1/2 cup	125 mL
Sliced green onion	3 tbsp.	50 mL
Grated lemon zest (see Tip, page 64)	1 tbsp.	15 mL
Salt	1/4 tsp.	1 mL

Combine water and salt in large saucepan or Dutch oven. Bring to a boil. Add pasta. Boil, uncovered, for 11 to 13 minutes, stirring occasionally, until tender but firm. Drain. Return to same pot. Cover to keep warm.

Heat olive oil in large frying pan on medium. Add mushrooms and garlic. Cook for about 5 minutes, stirring occasionally, until liquid is evaporated.

Add next 3 ingredients. Heat and stir until butter melts. Add scallops. Heat and stir for about 2 minutes until scallops are opaque.

Add remaining 4 ingredients and pasta. Toss. Makes about 6 cups (1.5 L).

1 cup (250 mL): 323 Calories; 10.4 g Total Fat (2.7 g Mono, 0.7 g Poly, 4.8 g Sat); 45 mg Cholesterol; 33 g Carbohydrate; 2 g Fibre; 23 g Protein; 419 mg Sodium

braised mushroom ragout

For those who are wild about mushrooms, this three-variety stew will have them demanding extra helpings. They'll never guess that this is low-fat. Serve with rice or crusty bread to collect every last drop of the flavourful gravy.

Package of dried porcini mushrooms	3/4 oz.	22 g	Put dried mushrooms into small heatproof bowl. Add boiling water. Stir. Let stand for about 5 minutes until softened. Drain. Chop. Set aside.
Boiling water	1 cup	250 mL	
Cooking oil	1 tsp.	5 mL	Heat cooking oil in large frying pan on medium-high. Add onion and garlic. Cook for 3 to 5 minutes, stirring often, until onion starts to soften.
Chopped onion	1 cup	250 mL	
Garlic clove, minced (or 1/4 tsp., 1 mL, powder)	1	1	
Sliced fresh white mushrooms	3 cups	750 mL	Add next 5 ingredients and reconstituted mushrooms. Cook for 5 to 10 minutes, stirring often, until carrot is tender-crisp.
Sliced portobello mushrooms	2 cups	500 mL	
Grated carrot	1/2 cup	125 mL	
Salt	1/4 tsp.	1 mL	
Pepper	1/8 tsp.	0.5 mL	
Prepared vegetable broth	2 cups	500 mL	Stir broth into cornstarch and thyme in small bowl. Add to mushroom mixture. Stir.
Cornstarch	1 tbsp.	15 mL	
Dried thyme	1/2 tsp.	2 mL	
Can of navy beans, rinsed and drained	14 oz.	398 mL	Add beans and spinach. Stir. Reduce heat to medium-low. Cook, covered, for about 5 minutes, stirring often, until boiling and thickened. Makes about 6 cups (1.5 L). Serves 4.
Box of frozen chopped spinach, thawed and squeezed dry	10 oz.	300 g	

1 serving: 225 Calories; 2.5 g Total Fat (0.8 g Mono, 0.8 g Poly, 0.3 g Sat); 0 mg Cholesterol; 39 g Carbohydrate; 11 g Fibre; 14 g Protein; 892 mg Sodium

mushroom thyme sauce

It's thyme you tried something different. Earthy mushrooms, beef broth and a touch of sherry result in a full-flavoured sauce that complements any type of pasta and is particularly good on gnocchi.

Package of dried shiitake mushrooms	3/4 oz.	22 g
Hot prepared beef broth	1 cup	250 mL
Butter (or hard margarine)	2 tbsp.	30 mL
Finely chopped onion	1/3 cup	75 mL
Thinly sliced fresh brown (or white) mushrooms	4 cups	1 L
Half-and-half cream	1/2 cup	125 mL
Dry sherry	2 tbsp.	30 mL
Chopped fresh thyme (or 1/4 tsp., 1 mL, dried)	1 tsp.	5 mL
Salt	1/4 tsp.	1 mL
Pepper	1/4 tsp.	1 mL

Put dried mushrooms into small heatproof bowl. Add hot broth. Stir. Let stand, covered, for about 15 minutes until softened. Strain liquid through sieve lined with triple layer of cheesecloth into separate small bowl. Reserve liquid. Thinly slice mushrooms, discarding stems if tough.

Melt butter in large frying pan on medium. Add onion, brown and shiitake mushrooms. Cook for about 10 minutes, stirring occasionally, until mushrooms start to brown.

Add half-and-half cream, sherry and reserved liquid. Bring to a boil. Reduce heat to medium-low. Simmer for about 10 minutes, stirring occasionally, until thickened.

Add remaining 3 ingredients. Heat and stir for 1 minute until fragrant. Makes about 1 3/4 cups (425 mL).

1/2 cup (125 mL): 156 Calories; 10.8 g Total Fat (2.9 g Mono, 0.5 g Poly, 6.7 g Sat); 30 mg Cholesterol; 12 g Carbohydrate; 1 g Fibre; 4 g Protein; 622 mg Sodium

recipe index

topical tips

Deep-fry temperature test: A deep-fry thermometer is an easy way to ensure the oil has reached the right temperature for crispy results. Failing that, you can insert the tip of a wooden spoon into the oil. If the oil bubbles around the tip, the temperature is correct. Or toss a bread cube into the oil. If it sizzles and browns in a minute, the oil is ready.

Roasting garlic on the grill: Slice 1/4 inch (6 mm) from the top of each bulb to expose the cloves. Wrap bulbs individually in greased foil and place on the side of the grill away from direct heat. Cook for 30 to 45 minutes until soft. Let stand until cool enough to handle. Leftovers can be wrapped and stored in the freezer.

Toasting nuts, seeds or coconut: Cooking times will vary for each ingredient, so never toast them together. For small amounts, place ingredient in an ungreased frying pan. Heat on medium for three to five minutes, stirring often, until golden. For larger amounts, spread ingredient evenly in an ungreased shallow pan. Bake in a 350°F (175°C) oven for five to 10 minutes, stirring or shaking often, until golden.

Zest first; juice second: When a recipe calls for grated zest and juice, it's easier to grate the lemon or lime first, then juice it. Be careful not to grate down to the pith (white part of the peel), which is bitter and best avoided.

Nutrition Information Guidelines

Each recipe is analyzed using the Canadian Nutrient File from Health Canada, which is based on the United States Department of Agriculture (USDA) Nutrient Database.

- If more than one ingredient is listed (such as "butter or hard margarine"), or if a range is given (1 – 2 tsp., 5 – 10 mL), only the first ingredient or first amount is analyzed.

- For meat, poultry and fish, the serving size per person is based on the recommended 4 oz. (113 g) uncooked weight (without bone), which is 2 – 3 oz. (57 – 85 g) cooked weight (without bone) — approximately the size of a deck of playing cards.

- Milk used is 1% M.F. (milk fat), unless otherwise stated.

- Cooking oil used is canola oil, unless otherwise stated.

- Ingredients indicating "sprinkle," "optional" or "for garnish" are not included in the nutrition information.

- The fat in recipes and combination foods can vary greatly depending on the sources and types of fats used in each specific ingredient. For these reasons, the count of saturated, monounsaturated and polyunsaturated fats may not add up to the total fat content.